THE STARTUP

LEAP YEAR

Go From Start To Great In

Your First Year of Business

Chris Bennett

ISBN: 0692953833
ISBN 13: 9780692953839
Library of Congress Control Number: **XXXXX (If applicable)**
LCCN Imprint Name: **City and State (If applicable)**

<u>Dedication</u>

This book is dedicated to my father, who gave me a front-row seat to being an entrepreneur, and to every organization whose purpose is to help business owners be successful.

Table of Contents

- o What is your ideal customer most passionate about?
- o What pains does your ideal customer have?

Step 6: Fix Your Approach

- Define Your Value Message
- Reaching Your Market
- Using the Right Marketing Channels
- Cost Effective Ways to Market Your Startup

Step 7: Go Shopping

- Shopping at Your Competition
- Recognizing Your Strengths and Weaknesses
- What Makes You So Special

Step 8: Launch Big

- Start with the End in Mind
- Build The Momentum
- Set Up Your Activity Calendar
- Sample Activity Calendar
- Take Massive Action and Proper Execution

Step 9: Keep Your Eyes on the Prize

- Stay Away from Distractions
- Prepare for the Inevitable
- Answer the Wake-Up Call
- Be Uncomfortable

__Introduction__

My story started when I came to the United States for college. I really just wanted to get away from my dad, who had been nagging me about what I was going to do with my life. While in my junior year in college, I got an internship with a car rental company. This was my very first job, and they groomed me to engage, interact, and sell to customers. After finishing college, I was accepted as a full-time employee and moved quickly up the management chain, mostly overseeing multiple offices. At the time, my dad was very ill, so I took time off to visit him in Jamaica. When I got there, he had to undergo surgery to remove his little toe because his blood wasn't circulating properly, which was caused by his diabetes. Soon after the doctors removed it, they realized his blood wasn't circulating past his knee, so they amputated his right leg. What should have been a three-month leave of absence turned into a year, after which my dad passed away. I was torn and upset, as well as lost. I came back to the States, hoping my big managerial position would be safe, but I came face to face with the fact that I had to start all over and work my way back up. This was a devastating blow. My bills had accrued to record levels, and I needed a stable and good-paying job. I started a career search and became a territory sales manager for an insurance company that had a different culture, and it was entirely different from what I was accustomed to. My transition from a big corporate giant to a medium-sized company wasn't easy, but I had no choice but to make it work. I became very unhappy because of the restriction placed on my area and on my potential to earn a living. Long story short, I got fired. On the drive home, I remembered how they had taken away everything that belonged to them, things like the company car and cell phone. They had someone drop me off at my home, and that same driver picked up my printer, which also belonged to them. I was relieved but, at the same time, fearful because I had no idea what was next. After a few days of panic attacks, of worrying that all my dreams would never come true, I had to dig deep and remind myself of who I was and of my potential. I asked myself two questions: What's the one thing I could do with an above-average skill? What subject matter did most people ask me about? The next morning, I started my own marketing business, and by three o'clock that evening, I got my first client. In my first month in business, I made more money that month by

working for myself; never had I received an equivalent paycheck

from working for a company. I never looked back.

Step 1: It Begins with You

From Great Ideas to Achieving Goals

Everything starts from a seed, an idea, a thought from inspiration—from pain, regret, or joy—all of which are life-changing emotions that we possess or experience. The day you think about starting your business is the day it actually starts to exist, but there's what I would call the "in between" stage, which can prevent most us from reaching our full potential as business owners and as individuals. Denzel Washington, one of the most prolific actors of our generation (and one of my personal favorites) was speaking to a small group of actors in a fraternity, and in his willingness to give back and share, he broke down what I believe is the first step to really achieving success: a person must clearly identify the difference between a dream and a goal.

He said, "Dreams without goals remain dreams and ultimately fuel disappointment. Goals on the road to achievement cannot be achieved without discipline and consistency."

Having the idea to start a business is noble; making the decision to be an entrepreneur is brave and courageous and takes guts to actually embark on the journey to achievement.

Do understand that life is not a bed of roses, and the stars in the sky won't align perfectly in your behalf. Thus, the hardest part of starting a successful business is actually just starting. When I started my business, I was excited and fearful all at the same time—excited because I knew that I was starting a new journey and that I was on a path to achievement and accomplishment.

Denzel would say that I was proud to know that whatever thoughts and ideas I generated were actually coming to fruition. I saw myself at the beginning of a puzzle, not knowing exactly how the next piece would evolve. I was fearful because I couldn't hold anyone else accountable but myself; moreover, I didn't have a secure paycheck coming in next week, and I felt so unstable and unsure, always feeling that failure was lurking in the shadows.

However, these emotions—which you may experience—push us to ask ourselves one question: Shall we sink or swim?

I chose to swim, and so did you if you started your business. At first, I was like a kid in a candy store, hoping for everything, trying anything, accepting anyone that would pay for services. I was like a reckless driver trying to find a bearing. What helped me greatly was when my friend Luke told me about the "mirror technique." The mirror technique is designed to build self-confidence. To practice this technique, you need a tall mirror. Position yourself in the center, look yourself in the eyes, and say boldly (or declare) who you are as a person, how successful you are as a business owner, and how you expect great things to happen.

When I first used this technique, I knew the highs and lows that were soon to come, but I wrote on a piece of paper who I was as a man and as a business owner and how successful I could be as an entrepreneur. I practiced this technique every morning. I still do it today.

Find Your Passion Spot

At the 2007 All Things Digital conference, Steve Jobs (former CEO of Apple Inc.) explained that the number one rule to success is to do what you love and that what you love is what you'll be most passionate about. He said, "You must have passion for what you're doing, because it's so hard that any rational person would give up. If you look at the ones who were successful, they loved what they did, so they could persevere when it got really tough, and the ones that didn't love it…quit."

The biggest mistake I see new business owners make is to start a business and then to invest time, money, and emotions to build something they really aren't passionate about. If you're reading this and saying to yourself that you don't know what your passion is or if you're now analyzing yourself and realizing that what you're doing is not your passion, don't jump the broom just yet. Entrepreneurship may be your passion in general, but every business owner has a specific passion spot. T. D. Jakes, senior pastor at the Potter's House Church, has hundreds of books, DVDs, and CDs, and he does multiple conferences and workshops and more. Perhaps you're wondering, so what does TD Jakes have to do with my passion? Many people may say he's doing so much from speaking, writing best-seller books, and composing CDs and DVDs, but all I see is a man operating in the fullest of his passion—which is to communicate. He's a great communicator, and the books, DVDs, CDs, conferences, and workshops are just channels of communication—or, in other words, channels of passion.

I didn't know exactly what my real passion was until five years ago. I made a decision that I would only do what I loved and that it didn't matter if it wasn't the most glamorous, sophisticated, or common thing to do. I knew deep inside that only by doing what I loved could I be the best at what I would do. I don't know anyone in any business or field who is the best at what he or she does and is not successful.

If you look at the people who we look up to as icons of success, you may notice that they have specific characteristics with doing what they love at the forefront. For example, playing basketball was, without a doubt, Michael Jordon's passion, and he became the best. His achievements go without question: five MVP Awards, ten All-NBA First-Team designations, nine All-Defensive First-Team honors, fourteen NBA All-Star Game appearances, three NBA All-Star Game MVP Awards, ten scoring titles, three steal titles, six

NBA Finals MVP Awards, and the 1988 NBA Defensive Player of the Year Award. (The list goes on).

In 1994, Jordon tried to replicate the same level of success in his playing baseball for the Chicago White Sox, and although he was a great athlete, he was an average baseball player. Most people don't know this, but his main reason for playing baseball was to honor his father's passing; his father had always envisioned him as a Major League Baseball player. Playing basketball was his passion spot, what he loved the most, and what he was the best at. Now, he holds quite a legacy.

Win Is Your Attitude

Zig Ziglar, one of the pioneers of our generation in sales and business motivation, said, "Your attitude, not your aptitude, will determine your altitude." Attitude is everything, and a winning attitude is even better. When you start your business, your attitude will determine how successful you become.

When I started my business, I was pumped, thinking that the world was mine and that all I had to do was go and get it—that was my attitude. I told myself that starting my business was going to be hard, but I was determined to do whatever it took to succeed; both of those concepts formed my core attitude.

Grant Cardone—a self-made millionaire, entrepreneur, and international sales speaker—has an infectious, winning, get-to-work attitude. In July 2014, I was at his office in Miami Beach, Florida, and I was quite inspired by the atmosphere of the "win attitude," which I saw not only in him but also in everyone who worked for him. His philosophy is that you have to "10X" everything you do, take massive action, and do whatever it takes to succeed. He even has a reality TV show called *Whatever It Takes.*

So how do you create your atmosphere of a winning attitude and keep it. The secret is you. John Maxwell says, "Everything rises or falls on leadership." When you become full of a winning, can-do attitude, you become infectious to the people around you and to potential customers.

Here's something that business owners often overlook: even customers like doing business with people with a winning attitude.

People like winners, and everyone wants to be on the winning team. Here's a news flash: you're a winner, and you're the captain of the winning team—never forget those things.

<u>Step 2": Beat the Fear</u>

The Fear Factor

We've all heard of Will Smith or grew up watching him on TV or in movies. *The Fresh Prince of Bel-Air*, *Bad Boys*, *I Am Legend*, the lucky guy married to Jada Pinkett Smith – Will Smith is no stranger to stardom, and now you're wondering, What does Will Smith have to do with "The Fear Factor"? On September 25, 2018, Will Smith decided to celebrate his fiftieth birthday by bungee jumping out of a helicopter over the Grand Canyon – yes, that's what I said, the Grand Canyon. He did something outrageous. In fact, it was crazy and dumb, but it was also powerful beyond measure. The world watched as he took his leap of faith and jumped. As he descended into the depths of the Grand Canyon, the adrenaline rush and fear of a life-ending accident hovered in the air. As he ascended from the jaws of the Grand Canyon, he shouted "From pure terror to absolute bliss." It was at this moment Will Smith realized how beautiful it was on the other side of fear. He later said to a group of supporters who had gathered to watch, "The hesitation is what messes up your dream."

Almost everyone who has decided to "jump" into starting their own business has had to face their fears. The fear of failure, the fear of success, the fear of yourself. You have to confront the reality that you have nothing to fear but fear itself.

When I started my business, it was the most fearful time of my life. I feared being broke and not being able to provide for my family, especially just after being fired from my corporate job. My confidence was at an all-time low. What if I wasn't good enough? What if no one bought my products or services? What if I couldn't provide for my family? It was as if someone had dropped me in the middle of the ocean with land just in sight and I had two options: accept fear and drown or have faith in myself and swim. If you believe, you swim!

I refer to being in a situation that forces a defined course of action as a "life-changing moment." After I decided to swim, it was as though I became possessed with a will to win, a will to live. And the more I swam, the more energy I had; the more I swam, the closer I could see landfall; the more I swam, the clearer it became that the only thing that had been holding me back was the lack of belief in myself.

What I learned is that whenever you're face to face with fear, one of two things occurs. The fear either cripples you or springboards you, and the people, friends, and voices in your life at that given moment have more to do with what happens to you than you think. This is why most successful entrepreneurs will tell you that staying away from negative people or counsel is essential for your business success. Having people around you who believe in you feeds your will to jump and succeed.

Understanding Fear

According to *Psychology Today*, "Fear is an emotional response induced by a perceived threat, which causes a change in brain and organ function, as well as in behavior." Most of our fears are the result of an emotional response to "What-ifs." What if my business fails and my wife leaves me? If you let them, these emotions will trigger a fear response – not wanting your wife to leave you for a richer, younger man – and of course fear never just remains constant; if left alone, it grows. If you are overwhelmed by fear, that fear starts to affect your actions, because your "What-ifs" are now as real as a heart attack. (Meanwhile, your wife has no idea she's in love with an imaginary boyfriend you and your fear erratically made up.)

When I try to understand fear, I ask myself questions such as, who told me as a kid I needed to be afraid of the dark? Why was I so afraid of "Chucky" (an emotional doll that had some serious anger management issues)? Why was I afraid to tell my dad when I got less than an A on my science project? My point is, even as a kid, fear presents itself in many ways.

Recently I went to a growth and investing conference my brother, Luke, hosted in the beautiful country of Trinidad and Tobago. It was an exciting time because not only did my brother host the event; he was also responsible for getting more than 5,000 people to attend. My brother at the time was one of the top earners – and perhaps still is, depending on when you read this – in a company called IML (International Markets Live). I saw him work tirelessly to grow his business and share his life-changing knowledge of financial investing and freedom.

At the event, Luke's mentor and now mine, David Imonitie, was the guest speaker. If you've never heard of David, his story is remarkable, and a true display of how belief in self, persistence, and hard work can transition you from dead broke to a self-made millionaire. I sat in the front row screaming my lungs out, cheering while David made his way to the stage to address this crowd of 5,000-plus attendees. His first words, I remember, came in the form of a request to the boisterous crowd of future entrepreneurs and millionaires. He said, "I want you to raise your hand if you see yourself making $83,333 a month." I kid you not, when he said this, it was like a gut punch from Iron Mike Tyson. TKO! Stop the fight! It was as if someone had knocked the air completely out of the room as a few people timidly raised their hands. He then repeated the statement, "Raise your hand if you see yourself making $83,333 a month." This time, around 50 percent of the audience raised their hands in growing belief. David then took a deep breath and shouted the same instruction a third time, "Raise your hand if you see yourself making $83,333 a month." At this point in the conference, if you didn't have your hand raised, you perhaps were going to be escorted out to join a rehabilitation program, but something happened.

Have you ever watched a movie where the scene freezes and only the main character can move or knows what's really going on? Well, that was me! I was the main character in the room of 5,000-plus attendees. I first saw doubt sneak into the room, which then opened the door for its cousin, fear. The first time David made his request, I saw the doubt and disbelief on people's faces, but as he continued to repeat the same instruction, I eventually saw belief step into the room and transform people's minds, then their expressions. And at that point I knew how to overcome fear.

You see, $83,333 a month equates to $1,000,000 a year. David was testing the audience to see whether they believed, because he knew, as the saying goes, "If you believe it, you can achieve it." He had to build their confidence and belief to a place where every person within themselves could say confidently three things:

I can see it.

I can do it.

I believe it's possible.

Overcoming Fear

According to Entreprenuer.com, there are three ways you can overcome your fear:

1. Rewrite Your Brain
2. Have a Well-Thought-Out Plan
3. Do One Thing Every Day That Scares You

Rewrite Your Brain

To rewrite your brain is, I believe, simply to look within and tell your inner self, "I believe in you. You can do this." And you believe this so much it becomes your reality. To rewrite your brain, you need a supporting case, great inspirational books and videos, success stories, mentors who walk the walk not just talk the talk, and most importantly great friends. To rewrite your brain, you must be constantly aware of your input, because what you put in is what you'll put out.

In going through this same exercise, to rewrite my brain, I initially wrote down on a piece of paper who I was, the commitment I was making to myself, and what I was willing to do to achieve my goals. I memorized what I had written, and every morning in front of the mirror I looked myself in the eyes and repeated it until it stuck – or until my brain got rewritten. Also, throughout my day, I constantly listened to my mentors talk about staying focused and getting the most out of every day. Rewriting your brain is a lot like eating: you must feed your belief every single day.

Have a Well-Thought-Out Plan

In 2016, I launched the business planning division of my company, specifically focused on developing strategic business plans to help business owners start, launch, or grow their business and to access the funding they needed. I did this because I realized how important it is not just to believe, but to have a solid, strategic plan of action, like a guide toward becoming successful. When most people think of a business plan, they believe it's a bunch of nice words and some figures that are made up and that it's something you do once and then forget. Instead, a business plan is like an instruction manual for how to build a newborn baby's crib from scratch. If the instructions are good and you can follow the directions, you'll be able to complete the task successfully before your newborn arrives. A solid plan gives you the confidence and reassurance you need that you can do this, and when you're doing it, you're staying on the right path. A solid plan of action should always be clear and have goals with dates to mark your achievements.

A good friend of mine was venting to me about how unsettled she felt about her boyfriend leaving his job to start his own business. For many wives or significant others, this fear of lack of income or change can be a worrisome experience, but in this case I discerned that income or change wasn't the real underlying issue that was bothering my friend. After talking some more with her, I realized the issue wasn't that she was afraid of her boyfriend not having a steady income or of the change of direction from corporate big shot to entrepreneur; it was more about her lack of belief in him. If it looks like a duck, swims like a duck, and quacks like a duck, then it's hard to say that it's not a duck. Unfortunately, in this case, her boyfriend wanted to be a duck without all the attributes and features that define all ducks.

I asked her what she would need to see her boyfriend do in order to believe in him, and what she said was really telling. She said, "I need him to get out of bed earlier than nine in the morning. I need him to act like he believes in himself. I need him to act like this business idea is not just an idea. I need him to do the necessary research and set a thirty-, sixty-, and ninety-day plan of specific daily actions targeted at achieving specific short-term goals. I need him to not be a joke."

This could be many people's story. As for my friend's boyfriend, I'm not sure whether he ever started his business, but what was clear to me through her experience, from her different perspective of being the other person, was that it's important to be a duck. It's important to have a solid plan broken down into specific daily actions.

Do One Thing Every Day That Scares You

Being comfortable is the fastest and easiest way to fail at growing

your business. When we constantly do what's easy or do just

enough, we inadvertently create a comfort zone within which we set

our targets and limitations. I was listening to Dan Lok, a very

successful entrepreneur, investor, and coach, explain his interesting

theory of the comfort zone. He first asked his listeners to imagine

themselves drawing a circle and within that circle to write down

everything they had in life right now. He then asked them to draw

outside the circle everything they wanted in life but didn't have. This

circle, Dan explained, is our comfort zone, and in order to get what

you don't have, you have to stretch and expand your circle or

comfort zone. I distinctly remember him saying, "The number one

habit you need to be successful is to consistently on a daily or

weekly basis do things that make you feel uncomfortable."

The first business I started was a digital agency that I ran from home,

and it was reasonably successful. I had low overhead and personnel

expenses. Most of the work I could do myself. I outsourced overseas

to increase my margins, and most of my business came from

referrals and people I knew who gave me a chance to grow their business. When I was starting out, because I knew my overheads where so low, I intentionally kept my prices low so that I could ramp up repeat clients on six- to twelve-month contracts, after which the plan was to redefine my target base by focusing on acquiring a specific customer group that would pay more and have better retention. Eventually, I had to hire a few permanent team members, but I clearly remember when the business reached its ceiling and no matter what I did, I couldn't seem to pass a certain number of clients. I was frustrated, working harder than when I started and growing less. I was playing defense not offense with new sales, and it was killing me inside. In my efforts to fix this stunted growth, I invested thousands of dollars visiting growth conferences and seminars, and although the information was great, nothing worked for me. I remember praying one night, asking God to send a business angel to save me. I know you think I'm being funny right now, but I was dead serious. My business growth was my livelihood, and I saw it dying.

After stressing out for weeks about my business issue, which was increasingly becoming a personal one, while scrolling on Facebook, I saw a video post by Grant Cardone entitled "Next Level." This was an immediate attention grabber for me, because at this point, I was so desperate, I wanted to believe in anything hopeful that would save my business. In fifteen seconds, I kid you not, I got my first aha moment. Grant said, "You're one skillset away from going to the next level." I paused for a bit while this sunk in. I was still listening when he said, "You know that one thing you avoid doing, that you put off to do last, that thing that makes you so uncomfortable … do it first every day and do it so much until you love it." In thirty seconds or less, I was unstuck, because I now knew what I had to do. What I had to do to take my business to the next level was to simply get on the phone and find who had my money.

I hated prospecting! It was extremely uncomfortable. I would rather send one thousand emails and respond to one hundred direct messages than make one cold call. I recall struggling to do this the next morning, but I remembered and repeated the commitment I had made to myself, "I will do whatever it takes to become successful," and so I did it, rejection after rejection. What ended up happening after my first week was that I wasn't so uncomfortable cold calling; the stronger my prospecting skill got, the easier it became, and the more I started to enjoy the phone. I remember making my first sale and it felt good, it felt real good, because at that moment I knew my business had just moved to the next level.

Step 3: Get a Plan

Defining Your Vision

One of the most critical first steps in starting your business is clearly defining your vision. Most companies do this in the form of a vision statement that they use as a constant reminder of the primary direction of the company. Three examples of successful company vision statements are:

> **Nike:** "To bring inspiration and innovation to every athlete in the world"

> **Starbucks:** "Our mission: to inspire and nurture the human spirit – one person, one cup and one neighborhood at a time"

> **Amazon:** "Our vision is to be Earth's most customer-centric company; to build a place where people can come to find and discover anything they might want to buy online"

Note that the one thing that stands out after reading all three vision statements above (Nike, Starbucks, and Amazon) is that none of them comes as a surprise. Each of these companies, a giant in its own right, has kept to its vision statement because it forms its identity and culture as an organization.

Having a twenty-year vision statement when starting your business might seem a little far-fetched. You might be thinking you'll be lucky if you can see past three years. Vision statements can change over time; as a company grows, so does its vision. Some visions become even bigger as the company realizes a greater social and economic responsibility.

When starting your business, your vision statement should be founded firmly upon answering the following question: "How does the company intend to stay true to its beliefs while helping as many people in the best way the company knows how?" I believe answering this question will help you strategically create and develop the vision statement for your company.

The Right Business Model

What's so paradoxical for me is the fact that the biggest taxi service in the world owns zero cars. Think about that. I'm talking about the most disruptive and innovative company within the last decade, whose recent success has changed the way economists and financial gurus look at business models today. The taxi service I'm referring to here is a company called Uber.

According to Investopedia, "Rumor has it that the concept for Uber was born one winter night during the conference when the pair [Travis Kalanick & Garrett Camp] was unable to get a cab. Initially, the idea was for a timeshare limo service that could be ordered via an app. After the conference, the entrepreneurs went their separate ways, but when Camp returned to San Francisco, he continued to be fixated on the idea and bought the domain name UberCab.com." The rest is history.

The true beauty, I believe, about Uber is that as a fellow entrepreneur, I can just picture myself being either Travis Kalanick or Garrett Camp (co-founders of Uber) with a brand-new idea. I can just imagine how many ideas these guys get on a daily basis, but that feeling – that this one is a winner – is almost equivalent in my books to buying a lotto ticket and just knowing this is it. I strongly believe that neither Kalanick nor Camp could have predicted the rampant growth Uber has seen, but that's the power of choosing a business model that is cost effective and super scalable.

When you're starting out, depending on your industry and financial goals, there are a few business models that you could select from. I've paired each business model with a well-known company that is currently successfully using it. This table will give you an idea how you can best select the business model that will fit your business.

Model	Company	Benefits
The Middleman	Warby Parker	Offers great pricing advantage and saves consumers money
The Marketplace	Airbnb	Zero or no overhead or no inventory
Subscription	Dollar Shave Club	Great balance of value to both the startup and the customer
Customized Everything	Black Lapel	Increasing interest in built-to-order products
On-Demand	Uber	More cost effective and scalable
Modernized Direct Sales	Amway	More people are seeking to supplement their income
Freemium	LinkedIn	High customer comfort levels to try your service
Reverse Auction	eBay	Attracts a lot of price-sensitive buyers
Virtual Good	Candy Crush	Allows you to create real value with high margins

Choosing the Right Mentor

Choosing the right mentor is, I believe, one of the most overlooked and underrated aspects not just of starting a business, but also of being successful in your first year. In terms of achieving your goal of business success, having a proven mentor on your team has tremendous value. I get worked up whenever I talk about mentorship, because that is the number one regret I have about starting my first business. When I look back at all the failures, all the money wasted, all the setbacks and disappointments, the many times I had to start over because I lacked the foresight to scale my business, it all could have been avoided if I'd had a mentor starting out. Although the experience I've gathered over the years has made me what I am today and has put me in a position to help so many people, I can't help asking myself these questions: What if I'd had a mentor when I started out? How far ahead would I be? What advice would I give my younger self if I had the chance?

A great part of my passion for writing this book is to offer mentorship advice and give to you what I couldn't give to myself. While having a mentor is important, not all mentors are equal and not all mentors are meant for you. Choosing the right mentor is critical in being successful in your first year of business.

Hopefully I've hammered home how important mentorship is, so let's talk about how to find the right mentor for you.

Self-Discovery

Before picking a mentor, you need to understand who you really are. Unraveling and understanding your abilities, character, and what you lack is critical to this process. Self-discovery helps a person figure out who they are, identify their weaknesses, and thereby embrace what they should improve on. After going through this process of self-discovery, you will be able to choose a mentor who is willing to help you achieve what you lack.

Honesty

Honesty is an important attribute during self-discovery and in choosing a mentor. Individuals must be honest with themselves to determine what they are truly lacking and what is crucial to them. Without honesty, it will be difficult to find the right mentor who deserves enough respect to be able to help.

Specificity

The mentor you choose must be specific to your goals. If you are a marketer, for example, a scientist will not make a good mentor for you. Choose a mentor expert in your objective if you really desire excellence.

Track Record

Track record refers to past failures, achievements, and performance – which add up to an individual's reputation. As an entrepreneur you need to research the track record of your desired mentor. Once you find out what records of excellence a person has set, it will be easy to figure out how they can help you. Reviewing a prospective mentor's past accomplishments is a good way of discovering who their connections are. Your mentor's connections can also become part of your network.

Network

Networks are important to making it as an entrepreneur, but you must choose the right connections in order to prosper. Mentors can help you make proper connections, and you should ensure that whoever you choose as a mentor is in the same line of business as you. This way, the mentor can connect you directly to important people in their network – or at least provide a way you can contact them.

Availability

Strangely, most people choose mentors without considering their availability. Is the individual able to communicate with you, or did you just say that a person is your mentor because you know a lot about them? Remember that there is a difference between a person you admire and a mentor. Whoever you choose should be available to chat with you electronically, as they may not be able to meet face to face whenever you need them. Mentors also have businesses to focus on and will, therefore, not stop to help with yours. Availability means having some time to answer your emails, respond to calls, or reply to messages. If a person cannot do this, then they are not a suitable candidate. A mentor must be able and willing to help in your entrepreneurial journey, making sacrifices to pull you out of the mud and spur you on. They should never hesitate to respond to your requests for help in reaching your full potential. In short, a mentor must be available to you whenever you are in need of their opinion,

suggestions, criticism, or praise.

Step 4: Get Unstuck

There is a place I call the "In Between" that I tell new business owners to be cautious of. It's like the twilight zone of business. This is the place where you make just enough revenue not to quit, and not enough to keep growing. It's like finding out your business is in quicksand, becoming stagnant and sinking. I'm a firm believer that if your business isn't growing, it's dying, and without some of the tools and insights in this book, I believe a lot of new business owners will find themselves lost and trapped in the "In Between" for a long time or forever.

When I started my digital agency, it was an exciting time. SEO (search engine optimization) wasn't so competitive, and most businesses were not already burnt from contracting overnight SEO gurus who produced no results. I had a lot of fun consulting for clients on the SEO process and seeing them close new business from our efforts. As the market became more saturated, the level of expertise dwindled and more companies began to experience the burden of high investments with little or no return. My "In Between" moment came when I realized as a growing digital agency that I couldn't pass the thirty retainer client threshold. Whenever I got to thirty clients, I would lose five. My business was stuck, to say the least, and to make things even worse, I had an issue collecting money. I felt as if I was slowly sinking. I had to ask myself these questions: Why was I losing customers? Why wasn't I growing past thirty clients? In answering my own questions, I reflected on the time when I had only fifteen clients. I was more responsive in my communication. I had more time to dedicate to getting my clients results. And because I had consistent open communication and met my clients' performance expectations, I had no issues collecting money on time each month. This was when it hit me like a ton of bricks that I had three major challenges that needed urgent attention.

The first challenge: business process

When I started my agency, it was from a small room in my house. I was a one-man army. I did the prospecting, appointments, closing, operations, and project management, and for the first ten to fifteen clients it was fine. But as I grew the one-man-army business model, my business began to shut down, because it wasn't built to perform past fifteen clients. The more clients I got, the more operational issues would arise; my front end was amazing, but my backend operations and fulfillment were a mess. It was time for me to expand my team and have a documented front- and backend process in order to grow my business.

The second challenge: service delivery

Losing a client is hard to stomach, especially when you're starting out and every client counts, but I believe these are great learning opportunities to grow your business. Therefore, I strongly recommend you conduct "exit interviews" when you lose a customer. When a client has nothing more to lose, you'll get the real reason they decided to break the partnership with you. I must warn you, the feedback you get may not be pleasant; in most cases, it's blunt, dry, abrasive, and borderline disrespectful, but if you can stomach this and read between the lines, the gems are remarkable.

I once had a client whose name was Yuri. She had an international shipping business, and she depended on international traffic to drive her shipping orders from the United States. This was a first for us. We'd never had an international client before, and the challenge posed to us – to figure out how we could drive international traffic – was alluring. The first mistake we made was that we didn't do extensive research. The second mistake was that because of the lack of detailed information we gathered, we set poor expectations with Yuri. The third mistake was that when we finally figured out how to meet and exceed our client's expectations, it was too late because we had lost credibility and trust. In our exit interview with Yuri, she told us, bluntly, "You guys failed us. You guys cost us." Up to this day, this experience affects me, but it taught us a valuable business and life lesson: "Never be anyone's guinea pig." What we should have done was tell Yuri upfront that we had no experience driving international business and that we'd do our research to ensure we had a successful blueprint to meet her expectations or advise if they were unrealistic. As I said, exit interviews are great learning tools.

The third challenge: access to funding

Between paying personal bills and supporting my family, while losing customers and having an increasingly late or nonpaying clientele, my business was in desperate need of additional funding. We needed a quick cash injection, and I had no idea where to turn. I thought about asking a friend for a loan, but it was too embarrassing to ask; my pride wouldn't let me. After all, I was supposed to be the guy with the successful business who had the world at his feet. So I started to look for alternative options to get financing. I called my bank to inquire about getting a loan, but they mentioned that I had to be making two hundred and fifty thousand a year and to have been in business for at least two years. Since, at the time, I had only been in business for eighteen months, I automatically didn't qualify. I turned to short-term lending companies, and although they offered immediate solutions, they would also have compounded my existing problem. The interest rates I was being offered would basically bankrupt me or put me in a cycle of continuously borrowing money. In my frustration at not seeing a real solution, I decided to become vulnerable and start talking to other business owners who were in my industry and asking them whether they had experienced what I was going through and whether they had any suggestions that could help me.

To my surprise, they had all had to borrow money, but there was one main distinction: They had great credit, and I didn't. Because they had great credit, they had access to financing on favorable terms as well as multiple lines of credit to sustain their business. My credit was something I always meant to improve, but I never had the time or saw the urgency because I had already bought a house and didn't feel it was that important. I couldn't have been more wrong! From this experience I learned a few valuable lessons.

First lesson: Don't be afraid or feel embarrassed to ask for help or advice from trusted sources. Second lesson: Banks don't lend money to desperate companies. Third lesson: Join a network of industry partners; their insight can prove to be invaluable. Fourth lesson: Invest in having great credit.

How I eventually solved all three business challenges was to cut back severely on personal and business expenses. I rented out my house and downsized to an affordable apartment, stopped eating out, focused on developing my backend business process while focusing all my energy on improving communication and service delivery to my remaining existing customers, and invested all those savings into improving my credit. Within eight months, I had great credit, a strong business credit line, and most importantly a core clientele with a business process that focused on an enriched customer experience. My recommendation to any new business owner is to ensure their credit score is 680-plus before starting their business and/or to make this a first-year priority goal.

Step 5: Find "JOE"

Defining Your Target Market

I love asking business owners the question, who exactly are you marketing to? Most people seem so confident when answering, because they feel that they have this question all figured out. I normally hear phrases like *anyone who* or *everyone with*. First, let this be a rule in marketing: the words *anyone* and *everyone* are a big no! What you're really saying when you start describing your target market with such words is that you're planning on wasting money. John Wanamaker said it best: "Half the money I spend on advertising is wasted; the trouble is I don't know which half."

When just starting your business, you can't afford to waste money on marketing campaigns that don't work, nor can you leave 50 percent of your marketing budget unaccounted for. The best way to improve results or conversions, as we marketers like to say, is to market, with a laser-like focus, to a target audience; to accomplish this, you first need to know who your ideal customer is.

Finding Your Ideal Customer

Have you ever said to yourself, "If I could get more customers like Joe, I would be fine"?

I just felt a light bulb go off. Joe is your ideal customer, and of course I'm just using Joe for the purpose of this book. It's almost a universal principle that rich people have rich friends and that smart people like to hang out with other smart people. Let's take this opportunity to analyze "Joe." The reason why we need to do this is because if Joe is your ideal customer, then Joe is your key to unlocking how to find and keep that type of clientele. These are the questions you need to ask yourself about finding your ideal customer:

1. What is your ideal customer's gender?

You may realize that a majority of your customers are predominantly either male or female or an even mixture of both.

2. What is your ideal customer's age range?

The product or service you offer will have a target age range because it will appeal more to the need of a specific type of person. For example, the new *Grand Theft Auto* game just came out for PlayStation. If I had to make a professional guess, I would say the age range would be from twelve to thirty-five; compare that with the age range of the new QuickBooks software, which is twenty-two to sixty-five. My numbers may be a bit off, but you get the point.

3. What is your ideal customer's geographic location?

You may realize that a majority of your customers live in specific countries, cities, or even zip codes. For example, if you're a personal-injury lawyer licensed with the Florida Bar, you're restricted to doing business in Florida only. Also, if your physical location is in Orlando and 98 percent of your customers come from within fifty miles of your location, then you have just pinpointed your geographical target area that converts for you best.

4. What is your ideal customer's main language?

Your business may be in Hialeah, Florida, where over 80 percent of the business and people speak only Spanish. Or your product may originally come from Latin America and may attract that market mainly.

5. What is your ideal customer's average income?

Knowing what your ideal client's average income is will definitely help you define whether someone is a potential ideal customer. This is highly contingent on the type of product or service. For example, if you were in the auto-dealer business and you were in a geographical area where the average household income was below $60,000, selling Bentleys and Maserati's would not be a good idea. On the other hand, if your dealership changed geographical locations to an area where the average income per household was about $500,000, it would definitely see bigger returns.

6. What industry is your ideal customer from?

If you're in the B2B line of business, this is extremely important: certain industries may have a bigger need for your services or products or may come in contact with your ideal customer. For example, ADP (automatic data processing), which is a global provider of integrated computing and business outsourcing, targets accountants specifically.

7. What is your ideal customer passionate about?

Your goal as a new business owner is to find the people who would be most passionate or interested in your product or service. For example, young golfers are very passionate people, and they are often so eager to improve their game. If you offered golf lessons or sold beginner-level golf clubs, this would be the market most passionate to buy your products or services. I'm passionate about marketing, so if I see a cutting-edge marketing book or new software, I become an impulsive buyer. Your product or service should make your ideal client more impulsive.

8. What pains does your ideal customer have?

You need to know what problems your ideal customers have; this is the only way you will remain relevant in their eyes. They have problems, and you have the solutions—that simple concept is business 101. If your product or service isn't solving anyone's problems or soothing anyone's pain, you won't be in business very long, sad to say. As a matter of fact, you didn't even start. For example, I help business owners to generate more leads and to convert more customers. Their pain is that they don't have either the time or the expertise to market their businesses effectively to get results. That's where I come in—I'm the pain reliever.

Step 6: Fix Your Approach

Define Your Value Message

I'll never forget my Advertising 102 class, when my college professor, Dr. Pellegrino, asked the question of war: Which is better, Coke or Pepsi? There was an immediate divide in the classroom, as if it were the red sea. No one was allowed to be undecided; everyone had to choose either Coke or Pepsi. At this point, I'm going to refrain from telling you which side I fought for. Just know that whatever side you're currently on, I'm right there with you.

When all was said and done and everyone was dressing their wounds, Dr. Pell said something that no one had heard before: "Do you know that the only difference between Coke and Pepsi is that one has more bubbles and the other more sugar?" Of course, the war started again.

That day, I fell in love with marketing because I had learned one of the most valuable lessons in life and in business: perception is reality. And if perception is reality, how do you want to be perceived? And what is your perceived value from customers?

To develop your value message allows you to be perceived the way you want to be and adds value to your appearance. In other words, do I really want to hear what you're saying? Your value message should tell potential customers exactly what your product and service is about. Your value message should be the strategic solution to your target market's pain or problems. For example, consider Geico's message: "Everyone knows fifteen minutes could save you fifteen percent or more on car insurance." This message solves pain and offers a solution. Think about it. When you think about getting insurance online, you immediately picture yourself filling out endless online forms and waiting forever to get a response. In Geico's message, the company is saying the process only takes fifteen minutes and that you could save 15 percent. Another example is Enterprise Rent-a-Car; it claims to be "the company that picks you up." Think about it. If you need to rent a car, getting to a car-rental location can cause some pain. Enterprise's message offers a solution.

When developing your value message, really spend some time thinking about it because it will tell customers exactly who you are and what you have to offer. If I were you, I would review steps one and two and then locate three people who could be an ideal client. Ask them what problems they are having and how someone could solve those problems. Your doing this will help you formulate a value message that speaks loudly and clearly to your ideal customers.

At this stage, you're at the midpoint in our journey together. You now should know that it starts with you. You should understand who Joe is and understand the importance of having a value message that speaks loudly and clearly. If you're a bit confused about what I'm talking about, you need to stop reading here and go back and read steps one through three. To follow these steps while effecting your startup business is extremely important because each step has a lesson to be learned. If you ignore those lessons, you will hinder your growth and development in the next levels. A wise man once said to me, "Some people go to school for years—whether a school of life or school of business—but spend it all repeating the same grade."

At this stage, you need to focus on answering three questions: How am I going to reach my market? What marketing channels will convert best? How can I automate this process?

Reaching Your Market

First, you need to define what marketing approach would work best for your business. There are three main types of approaches you can take—direct, indirect, or non-sales-force approaches—to reach your audience.

A *direct approach* involves using a direct sales force that interacts face to face with your target audience and usually focuses on penetrating a specific geographic territory. Although this approach is the most expensive (and I do not recommend this if you're just starting your business on a limited budget), it is known to convert the best. It does so because the ideal customers agree to meet the sellers in person, making it easy to expose the ideal customers' pains and positions toward the relative products or services, which then can lead to developing the appropriate solutions. When you start your business, I recommend that you be the sales force, become the face of the company, and establish your brand and sales culture before you bring in anyone else at this step. Your future success will be contingent on the reputation you can develop for your business during the last step, and you will be the business and your reputation will be constantly on the line. This is exactly what I did when I started my business: I tried to see many people that resembled my ideal customer. I knew if I could see at least eight potential customers a week who genuinely needed my services, I would at least convert two customers a week and would later show my sales team how to do the same, thus converting even more clients.

Second, the *indirect approach* consists of using agents, distributors, retailers, and value-added partners to reach your market. After these outlets come in contact with your target audience, you can use their influence and relationships to convert sales or reach clients. In my business, I used value-added partners as strategic-alliance partners or as affiliate partners to refer my ideal clients to me, in return for a small commission or referral fee, depending on the type of partners and industries they represented.

Third, the non-sales-force approach includes the use of advertising, promotion, direct mail, online marketing, and television channels to reach your ideal customers. Many business owners use these approaches to reach clients at more-affordable rates. For example, a new insurance agent may use Internet leads to generate new business. A new online store would definitely need online marketing, advertising, or promotions to get new clients. If you're in the service industry, you may use Internet marketing to cold or warm call potential new customers to get more sales daily. The secret is to know not only what type of business or industry you're in but also who and where your target market is. What is more, you must use the right marketing channels that can reach and engage your ideal customers in the best possible ways.

Using the Right Marketing Channels

There are so many ways today to do marketing, from the yellow book to following your customers online with banner ads. I believe the main challenge that startups have today, outside of working on a limited budget, is to identify what type of marketing to use that will reach their target audiences, the marketing expertise needed to grasp their attention, and the ability to convert a lead into a sale. The marketing channel you use will determine whether you even get a chance to be successful. Choosing the wrong marketing channel can be devastating and expensive and will put you out of business, so please listen very closely to what I'm going to say. For this example, let's use Instagram (an online social platform that is heavily driven by pictures) and consider the context of using a non-sales-force approach.

Here's the scenario: You just finished law school, and you started your own practice. Your area of expertise is asset protection, probate, and wills. You know (after considering step two) that your ideal customer has an age range from thirty-five to sixty-five. Barbara—a close friend of yours, who runs an accessories and clothing store—told you about using Instagram because she's getting sales every day.

Do you (A) take whatever money you have and use Instagram to get the same success as Barbara or (B) choose a direct approach to focus your time and energy on trying to set face-to-face appointments with potential customers. Think fast—what is your answer?

Before you shout out any letter of the alphabet, I want you to understand why option B makes perfect sense. After analyzing Instagram's platform, *Business Insider* said that "over 90 percent of the 150 million people on Instagram are under the age of 35, which makes it an attractive platform for many apparel, entertainment, and media brands focused on the 18- to 34-year-old age bracket."

So if the audience on Instagram has an age range of eighteen to thirty-four and you know your ideal client has an age range of thirty-five to sixty-five, then using Instagram would be ineffective—not because marketing on Instagram doesn't work (clearly it works for Barbara), but because it just wouldn't convert your target audience. Why? They're not on Instagram.

What I do to quickly determine whether a marketing channel would convert well for my business is play a game I call "Think like your customer." I know that it sounds like a game that five-year-olds would play when their parents can't get them to sleep; seriously, though, put yourself in your customers' shoes, be a customer (not a business owner), and ask yourself the following three questions:

- Would I buy that product or use that service?
- Would I come here to buy that product or use that service?
- What's the easiest way for me to get what I want?

These questions will put you in the right frame of mind to help you in choosing what works and what doesn't. Another thing I do is simply to call someone in the same type of business (preferably on the other side of the country so it doesn't feel that the call is aiding any competition) and just ask, what's working for you? or, what marketing techniques have you realized that are bringing in new business? You may be shocked at what people say; often, it's the most simplest of things with a high work ethic.

Cost-Effective Ways to Market Your Startup

Blogging. To establish your brand and credibility, start blogging right now. The quickest way to get your ideal customers to take note of you is to write articles that provide unique, original content that they would find very resourceful. If you're blogging about valuable stuff, you'll build a reputation and brand that customers will follow.

Attend Social Events. Not all social events are equal; that's why I only go to the fun ones. Social events should be just that—social. However, social events can be a bit overwhelming for a startup, especially if it doesn't have any big clients or cool stories to share. My suggestions are to have a great elevator pitch that's cool and a bit mysterious, to be truly interested in what people have to say about themselves or business in general, to ask great questions, and to have fun. I can't tell you how many times I've gone to social events not wanting to get any new clients but walk away extremely profitable. What you need to always keep in mind is that people like to do business with people they like. Be likeable!

Set Up a Google+ Local Page. According to Google, "Eighty-One percent of all customers first search on Google before making a final buying decision." What this means is that you can't afford not to be found on Google. One of the easiest ways to be found on Google is to create a Google+ local page and to make sure to include the category of work you do. Also, provide a detailed description with specific keywords about your product or service, claim your listing, and ask happy customers to give you positive reviews on your Google+ local page. Then you'll start getting business. Local marketing is trending and is getting even more attractive because people are more likely to buy or do business within familiar territories.

Share an Educational Video. Video is the future. If you haven't noticed, the only things people notice these days are cool pictures and awesome videos. To share videos is a cool way of connecting with your audience and, if done right, will drive more leads than you ever expected. I know you want to know what's the secret technique, so here it is: What ten questions do you most frequently get asked? Think about it, and then write them down. Answers to these questions are what your customers are searching for when they search on Google, on forums, and, of course, on YouTube. Write an article of no less than five hundred words, and in it answer each question. Put it on your blog, and share it on Facebook and LinkedIn; you can even attach it to your e-mails. Last but not least, create a one-minute video of you answering each question; in the video, be engaging, don't forget your personality on camera, and be you. If you take the time to effectively educate your customers, you will increase your credibility and trust, and once you have those two together, the sales will come.

Give Speeches. If you're afraid of giving speeches, skip this technique. Many people find giving a speech one of the most terrifying things to do. To stand in front of a room with five hundred strangers staring at you is not most people's idea of having a great time. However, if you like speaking and you're comfortable addressing small or large groups of people, this is your secret weapon. This is by far my most effective technique because it allows me, within seconds, to establish my credibility and trust. What I love the most when I give speeches is that I give so much value, and I increase the appreciation of what I do to get results, ultimately exposing my genuine passion for marketing. The best part is I don't have to sell—my passion does it for me.

Join a Networking Group. Networking groups are great for startups: they can put you immediately into a referral system that can generate new business. The challenge is to find the right networking group to join. The right one will have the following characteristics:

- Consistent attendance
- A system that holds members accountable
- A "givers gain" attitude
- Possible strategic-alliance partners
- High closed-business amounts from referred businesses
- Encourages social activity outside the chapter
- Respects your time
- Great leadership

Call Everyone in Your Phone. Word of mouth is still the best way to market your business. If you're in business and everyone in your phone doesn't know exactly what you do, stop reading this book and go and call everyone in your phone. To do so can generate immediate business and could create a consistent flow of referred business.

Participate in a Charity. Charities are a great way to meet decision makers and influencers. To be a part of a charity or worthwhile cause shows humanity and love for community. Customers like to support businesses or people who are making a difference. To be a part of a charity will shed insight about the character of your person and organization.

Play Golf. Many successful CEOs will tell you that some of their biggest and most-profitable decisions they have made were influenced by playing golf. I, on the other hand, can't elaborate too much, because I'm just beginning to learn the gracious game of golf. But trust me—play golf.

Answer the Phone. You can grow your business by 10 percent by simply answering your phone. I am amazed at how many times I have seen something on someone's website, called the relevant company, and no one answered. What was even more annoying was when they asked me to leave a message and then took five days to return my call—like who actually puts his or her entire life on hold to wait for a return call? I can't stress enough how many businesses lose potential customers because they don't pick up their phones. As a matter of fact, while developing your startup company, your attitude should be that you can't afford to miss one phone call.

You're always one phone call away from a big sale. Your phone is your lifeline.

Use Social Media. I'm just going to give you some social media stats so that you can come to your own conclusions whether this technique is important.

According to Buffer Social:

1. The fastest growing demographic on Twitter is the fifty-five to sixty-four age bracket.

2. One hundred eighty-nine million of Facebook users are "mobile only."

3. YouTube reaches more US adults aged eighteen to thirty-four than any cable network.

4. Every second, two new members join LinkedIn.

5. Social media has overtaken pornography as the number one activity on the web.

6. Ninety-three percent of marketers use social media for business.

It's clear—use social media to grow your startup...that's it!

Give Away Something for Free. Everyone loves the word *free*, but nothing in life is free, right? Use this technique to present to your ideal customers something that you know they would appreciate or use, and give it to them for free. The not-so-free part comes in when you use this free gift or offer as bait to lure them in and to capture their contact information, with which you can do follow-up phone calls or schedule meetings to generate new business. Remember, don't ever do anything for free, even if you're customers think so.

Step 7: Go Shopping

Shopping at Your Competition

Why shop at your competition? You need to because you have to know what you're up against. It's a cutthroat, dog-eat-dog race to the finish, and if you're not first, you're last. According to the website *Info Entrepreneurs*, "Knowing who your competitors are and what they are offering can help you to make your products, services, and marketing stand out. It will enable you to set your prices competitively and help you to respond to rival marketing campaigns with your own initiatives." Shopping at your completion is healthy for your business because it makes you aware of where you are, where you need to be, your strengths and weaknesses, and what works and what doesn't. What separates good salespeople and entrepreneurs from the world of average and mediocre is the zero tolerance they have for the competition and their knowledge of the FABs—the features, advantages, and benefits—of their products or services.

Early in my career at Enterprise Rent-a-Car and as a branch manager, I had to know what Hertz and Avis were doing all the time. I mean that it was a constant news feed. I had to know their prices, promotions, discounts, new car inventories, rental processes, and when they were short on cars. We even phone shopped them and pretended to be customers to get more information to use to our advantage, and (of course) they did it to us as well. This is what you have to do to be and remain on top. If you're the one on top, never forget that there's always a line of people behind you, waiting to take your spot. You have to be constantly aware of your competitors and marketplace.

Recognizing Your Strengths and Weaknesses

In 2011, when I started my marketing agency, I went after anything that moved, feeling full of zeal and hunger for any type of business. I later recognized that my fervent searching wasn't the smartest way to conduct my business, but I remember the very first time I realized how important it was to know what our competitors were doing. I got a call from Fred, a buddy of mine, who was opening his new weight-loss clinic (Franchise), and he invited three marketing companies to interview for the job. Although Fred and I were old schoolmates, he made it clear I had to bring my A game to get his vote of confidence. I was prepared as usual. I had my lucky tie on and favorite suit, and as I approached the conference room where the interview was going to be conducted, I felt like superman—indestructible and unstoppable. I didn't even knock on the door. My confidence turned the doorknob and busted the door wide open. When I got into the room, I saw what the other marketing companies had presented. They had custom-designed handouts and world-class, custom-designed presentations tailored to the customer. They had long lists of references to show, as well as seemingly cocky attitudes. No one told me that I was walking into a big ball of kryptonite. It was as if it were my first day in the major leagues; it seemed that what used to work in the minors would get me crushed. I had to think fast—I had to be quicker than Usain Bolt. I had to recognize what might strengths and weaknesses were and use my strengths against my competition.

At the time, my weakness was my presentation and a short list of references. My strengths were my passion for what I did, my dedication to partnerships, and my being more than just a sales executive—I was the person who had the skill set to actually perform what was necessary to get client results. Knowing this, I started the meeting by saying, "Gentlemen, not everything that glitters is gold. If you're looking for a marketing agency to get you more impressions, then that clearly is not me. But if you're looking to get more conversions, then I need your undivided attention."

With an opening line like that, I had the meeting all wrapped up, but it was my ability to properly educate and strategically show a tactical action plan that gave Fred the confidence to say, "This is our guy." I used my strength to overcome my weaknesses and outshine my competitors.

Although, I was happy to land my first sizeable account, it was an eye opener because my weakness was left exposed. So I used my competitors to mark the level of presentation I needed to start presenting to my potential clients; at the same time, I stuck to my strengths, focusing on being strategic, educational, and tactical.

What Makes You Special

Most of us have competitors who offer the exact same services and products, so a reasonable question to ask ourselves is, what makes me special? Why would a customer go to you versus going to your competitor or visa versa? If you can figure this out early, you'll fast forward your business success by five years. I once asked an insurance agent (my friend Brenda) this same question—that is, what made her special. Do understand that the insurance industry is by far one of the most competitive in our nation. In Brenda's case, because of where her agency is located, she has about ten competing local insurance agencies within a ten-mile radius. She was puzzled by the question because every time she suggested something that made her special, I responded with "and so do your competitors."

She said, "We are the best."

I said, "Your competitors say the same things and even write those things on their stores' front windows."

She said, "Well, we have the best companies."

I said, "Your competitors have the same companies and more than you do."

She quickly realized what my point was, and I saw a look of disappointment come across her face, as if she were thinking, I'm really not special, am I? At that point, I had to interject. I asked, "Do you want to know what makes you special?"

She said, "Yes, please tell me."

I said, "Do you really want to know what separates you from everyone else?"

She said, "Yes, tell me."

I said, "Do you want to know what's the one thing your customers can't get anywhere else but from you?"

She said "Yes!" for the third and final time.

I paused, held my stare, and said, "You."

You—yes, you—are the one thing that potential customers cannot get anywhere else. Your specific background, set of experiences, knowledge, personality, genuine care, and sincerity are what come across and are perceived by your clients as great customer service, trustworthiness, and credibility—all of which ultimately make you special and unique. For example, Brenda, our insurance agent, has a long history of being in the mortgage industry and offers more credibility and industry knowledge, both of which greatly benefit her customers seeking homeowners insurance. Even though there are ten competing insurance agencies within a ten-mile radius—and even though they are appointed to write with the same home-insurance companies—she's the only one that can provide in-depth knowledge that mirrors the mortgage and insurance industry and can present outside-the-box solutions that will benefit her customers. This is called finding your "unique marketing advantage."

Step 8: Launch Big

Start with the End in Mind

This is the most important step in this entire book because all you have learned—all the knowledge you have gathered up to this point about marketing your startup successfully—means absolutely nothing unless you become active. It's like having acquired mass knowledge and very little wisdom. We have heard many times over that "life rewards action"; this saying is true because no one ever achieved a dream by sitting on a coach or by just reading a book. Just reading this book won't make your business successful, and just reading the Bible won't make you a better person. My point is that it's what you do with knowledge that will determine your success and accomplishment in any area of your life, be it financial, entrepreneurial, or spiritual. No matter what, just get active.

One of the best ways to be constantly active is to do what Stephen Covey recommends: "Start with the end in mind." Visually imagine your end result, and then work backward, making yourself aware of all the activity you need to do to accomplish your goal. So if you're

a sales professional and your goal is eight closed sales a month, then

ask yourself how many phone calls and presentations you need to

make to achieve that end result. Say that you have just started your

new business, that you have a killer marketing plan and strategy, and

that you have the biggest dream to become a media mogul, but

nothing will ever come to fruition if you do not get your head out of

the clouds and do whatever it takes to get the results you need to

achieve your goals. I can't stress this enough: the more active you

are, the more productivity you will see in your business. Set higher

goals for your business, make no excuses, and do whatever it takes

to achieve them.

Build the Momentum

You've waited long enough. You've done everything you need to do

prior to this moment. This is it – your adrenaline is off the charts; it's

time to tell the world what your business is and what you can do to

help them. You know who your target audience is, where they are,

what your value message is, and how to reach them. It's go time!

Call everyone in your phone: If you're serious about all the hard work you've invested up to this point, don't overlook the most powerful tool you have to reach people; it's right there next to you – your phone! Most people's phones might have between fifty and five hundred contacts on average.

Host an event: Consider planning a product or business launch event to officially announce the launch of your new business with a bang. A unique and well-tailored event can be an excellent way to top off months of solid marketing groundwork and act as the catalyst to push your business to an even wider audience.

Release your launch video: Video is an effective way to reach a mass audience at a reasonable cost. Most launch videos are designed to capture the attention of your audience while strategically sharing your value message to your future clients. If you're doing a launch video, make sure it has great production and sound quality and is no longer than sixty seconds.

Utilize the power of social influencers: Within the past few years, social influencers have proven to be an increasingly effective tool to market products and services. This makes sense because you're tapping into someone else's traffic and using their trusted brand to endorse and promote your new service or product.

Run a launch promotion: The main objective here is to start building your pipeline of potential new customers. Nothing excites customers more than a targeted promotion of great value to them at a reduced cost. Although you're giving away a lot of value for less, if done right this strategy can prove to be very profitable. First look at your profit margins and see how much you can discount your product or service; then identify upsell or cross-sell products that aren't discounted but will greatly complement the sale and add value to your new customers.

Set Up Your Activity Calendar

Your activity calendar is simply a visual guide that shows the amount and type of activities that will aid you on the road to achieving your goal. Starting with the end in mind, first highlight what you want to achieve. The activity calendar visually shows you how it's going to be done.

The goal of setting up an activity calendar is to clearly identify your scalable metric. In simple terms, you need to define what your sales goal is and determine what specific actions will be the result of each sale. For example, I figured out that for every fourth sales appointment I conducted, I would close one sale that month. So if my sales goal was eight new clients a month, then I would need to do a minimum of eight sales meetings a week and thirty-two meetings a month to reach my minimum goal of ten new clients a month.

Here's a basic example of my weekly activity calendar. My goal is to get a minimum of ten new clients a month by completing the following: holding ten sales meetings, visiting two networking groups, attending two social events, giving one public speech, making seventy to one hundred phone calls, and executing three hours of Facebook or LinkedIn private messaging per week. Please note that you're free to try what works for me, but you should create what works best for your type of business and industry, based on all the steps in this book.

Sample Activity Calendar

Time	Mon	Tue	Wed	Thur	Fri	Sat
8am-9am	Team Meeting	Send Out Emails	Send Out Emails	Networking Group Meeting	Sleep In	Sleep In
9am-12pm	Phone Blitz	LinkedIn/ Facebook Messaging	Sales Meetings	Sales Meetings	Blogging	Read up on Industry News
1pm-3pm	Phone Blitz	Sales Meetings	Networking Group Meeting	Webinar	Video Shooting	Read a Book
3pm-6pm	Phone Blitz/ Prepare For Next Day	Sales Meetings/ Prepare For Next Day	Sales Meetings/ Prepare For Next Day	Give A Speech/ Prepare For Next Day	Open	Open
After Hours		Social Event		Social Event	Happy Hour	

Take Massive Action and Proper Execution

In the book *The 10X Rule: The Only Difference between Success and Failure*, by Grant Cardone, he talks about instigating a mind-set to 10X the way you think and double your activity to greatly surpass your goals. He talks about becoming obsessed with overachieving, with doing more than what is required, so you can attain more than average expectations.

When I started my business, that's exactly what I did: I released my beast and went to work, knowing that cute shirts and reading books all day were not going to put food on my table. Only by executing what I had learned, by putting my knowledge into practice, would I be successful.

In the 2014 NBA Finals, the San Antonio Spurs was the better team—not because they had better players, but because they did not. That is, they had a better team, a better unit of players that could execute key instructions to the best of its ability. Taking massive action and proper execution will separate true champions—in life, in sports, and especially in business.

Step 9: Keep Your Eyes on the Prize

Stay Away from Distractions

At around 2:00 p.m. on a Monday, I was wrapping up a meeting with a prospective client in Boca Raton, Florida. We had gone past the allocated time and were just shooting the breeze, talking about the Miami Heat and LeBron James's decision to move back to the Cleveland Cavaliers, when I suddenly realized that my alarm hadn't gone off for my second meeting, which started at 4:00 p.m. but in Greater Downtown Miami. I wasn't too startled, because it normally took me one hour to drive from Boca Raton to Miami via the I-95 Highway. So off I went, cruising on the I-95 at around half past two, when the traffic came surprisingly to a full stop. I checked my watch to make sure I wasn't caught in rush hour traffic, so I figured the traffic jam had been caused by a serious accident. After moving only five to eight miles in traffic for one hour, I started to panic because the one thing I hated to do was to cancel meetings by providing lame excuses, such as saying traffic was really bad. Those kinds of excuses don't really have…excuses.

I finally caught up to what I first thought was an accident, which only turned out to be two cops parked on the side of the road, having a friendly chat. I was pissed! And that's saying it lightly. However, in that very moment, right after I sped off after the bumper-to-bumper traffic magically disappeared, I learned a valuable life and business lesson. I learned that distractions will always keep you from achieving your goal in life and in your business. I know you're thinking that everyone knows that, but when the concept hits you like a ton of bricks, that's when it sticks. I immediately started to think about the things that were a distraction in my business—the things that kept me from reaching my goals: the "Hey, what's up dude?" phone calls (which took up one to two hours each day), the telemarketers that constantly called, the multiple social messages on Facebook that had nothing to do with work or with developing new business relationships, and many other distractions. The minute I started to guard my time and treat it as if it was the most precious commodity—which, in fact, it was—my business productivity, sales, and results went to a higher level. I got more done in four hours than I had been getting done in a whole day's work—just because I made a conscious effort to maximize my time and stay away from distractions. So the lesson of the day is to stay focus, to keep your eyes on the prize, and to stay away from anything that distracts you from your goals or slows your productivity. Michael Althsuler said it best: "The bad news is time flies. The good news is you're the pilot."

Prepare for the Inevitable

When I say, "Stay dirty," I don't literally mean to stay dirty (proper hygiene will be good for your business). What I really mean is that you should continue to put in the hard work and effort that you started out with and need to be successful. To every business with great potential, complacency is always its biggest enemy. Complacency is very patient. It waits for a false sense of security to creep in and keeps you back without you even realizing it until the IRS knocks on your door, but that's another story for another book. Complacency is like drinking a couple of rounds of dirty martinis, and then before you know it, you're being busted for a DUI. Or even worse, you suddenly find yourself in a fatal accident. Complacency is one of the devil's best friends; it's like a sheep in a wolf's clothes, something that you never see coming until it's too late. Andy Grove

said, "Success breeds complacency. Complacency breeds failure.
Only the paranoid survive."

Jack Welch said, "Change before you have to."

I am giving you so many examples and quotes because I hope that
they stick. If you follow these steps in this book, you will be
successful, and once that happens, you will have to face
complacency. In regard to that enemy, the only thing I can do to help
you is to prepare you for the inevitable.

Answer the Wake-Up Call

In my first six months after starting my business, I gave everything I
had, starting my days at 7:00 a.m., sometimes working until
midnight. I quickly got to a point where I felt comfortable. I could
pay my bills on time, go out and have fun with friends and family,
take my wife out on expensive dates, and have some money left over
for savings.

Thank God for wake-up calls, though. I lost three of my biggest
clients in one month. I started to lose focus on why I was in business
and what was truly important—servicing my clients and getting

them measurable results. I lost three of my top clients, which, at the time, were responsible for 50 percent of my business profits. In one month, I went from dining out twice a week and paying bills a week in advance to calling creditors and taking cooking lessons. It was a very humbling but necessary experience, which taught me to never take my eyes off what is truly important. I learned that things are never as bad *or* as good as they appear, which led me to understand that I must always keep my foot on the gas. I was lucky because my losing 50 percent of my business so early didn't put me out of business. Some people were not as fortunate as myself. I hope by sharing this that I have opened your eyes to how important staying focused and working consistently really are to running a business.

Be Uncomfortable

The only way to defeat complacency is to strive to be uncomfortable. Even saying it makes me feel uncomfortable. Say it with me: "I must be uncomfortable; my goal in business is to be and remain uncomfortable." You will remain uncomfortable when you set higher highs and increase your vision and goals, all of which will require more focus and effort. If you're comfortable where you currently are, your vision and goals are too small. You need to have a goal that frightens you and gives no place to false security and complacency. The biggest nugget that I got from studying millionaires and successful entrepreneurs was the fact that it wasn't about the money but more about being the best at what they did. To be the best takes discipline, focus, hard work, and, most importantly, consistency. You must never slow down, never take your eyes off the higher prize, never be average, and never allow yourself to be or feel satisfied. After all, if you're going to start a business, why not strive to be the best? If you're reading this book, it means there is something inside you that identifies with what I'm saying. If you apply steps one through seven, you will make leaps in fortune and success, from start to finish.

www.ingramcontent.com/pod-product-compliance
Lightning Source LLC
Chambersburg PA
CBHW020158200326
41521CB00006B/423